The Chelsea Centre Theatre Company presents
the world premiere of

Happenstance

by Pete Lawson

First performance at
the Chelsea Centre Theatre
8 June 1999

The Chelsea Centre Theatre Company presents
the world premiere of

Happenstance

by Pete Lawson

Cast (in order of appearance)

Neesh	Niki Mylonas
Lisa	Stephanie Pochin
Galina	Dilys Hamlett

Production Team

Director	Jacob Murray
Designer	Louise Wilson
Dramaturg	Mel Kenyon
Sound Designer	Francis Watson
Casting	Amanda Frend
Stage Manager	Caroline Batt

The Chelsea Centre would like to thank Guy Chapman, Marie-Louise Hogan, Jenni Hopkins, Susan Loppert and Melinda McDougall. The Chelsea Centre is a registered charity number 1060460.

DILYS HAMLETT

Theatre includes: Regional and repertory work at Royal Exchange Manchester, Edinburgh Festival, Nottingham Playhouse, York Theatre Royal, Watermill Newbury, Royal Theatre Northampton, Northcott Exeter, Theatre Royal Plymouth, Leicester Haymarket, Octagon Bolton including: **The Winter's Tale; The Deep Man; The Cherry Orchard; Hope Against Hope; Long Day's Journey into Night; Hayfever; Your Home in the West; Miss Julie; Little Eyolf; Hamlet; Old Times; Who's Afraid of Virginia Woolf; The Rivals; The Boyfriend; Pal Joey and Cleopatra; The Corn is Green; On Golden Pond; Road to Mecca; The Aspern Papers; In Praise of Love; Cold Comfort Farm; A Delicate Balance; An Inspector Calls; My Fair Lady; The Daughter in Law.**
In London: **Brand; A Passage to India; Peer Gynt; Othello; Measure for Measure,** Old Vic; **As You Like It; Romeo and Juliet,** Open Air Regent's Park; **Overboard,** Orange Tree; **Becket; Cyrano de Bergerac,** West End; **Becoming,** La Mama, New York; **Have You Anything to Declare,** Milwaukee Rep Co; **The Trial Of Joan of Arc,** Manchester and York Minster; **Honneger's St Joan,** Exeter; **Hamlet; Richard III** (1998), all RSC.
Television includes: **Pavlova; Twelfth Night; Uncle Vanya; Women of Troy; The Rainbow; No More Dying Then; The Moving Finger; Gaudy Night; Fire at Magillan; Harnessing Peacocks.**
Film includes: **The Wolves of Willoughby Chase; The Hollow Reed.**

NIKI MYLONAS

Theatre includes: **The Merchant of Venice; The Beggar's Opera; The Caucasian Chalk Circle,** Old Vic; **Macbeth,** Cockpit; **The Armitage Affair,** King's Head; **What the Dickens; Full Moon,** Southwark Playhouse; **Romeo and Juliet,** Holland Park; **Execution; The Hangman's Noose; Tales of Witchcraft; The Supernatural,** The Clink.
Radio includes: **Macbeth's Witches.**
Film includes: **The Vapour,** Light Source Productions; **Wrapped,** Mimosa Productions

STEPHANIE POCHIN

Theatre includes: **Direct from the Edge,** Kepow Theatre Company; **The Glass Menagerie; The Tempest; The Provok'd Wife; Blood Wedding,** all Mountview.

PETE LAWSON

For the Chelsea Centre: **Burning Houses**
Theatre includes: **The Impostor,** English language adaptation of Moliere's **Tartuffe,** Plymouth Theatre Royal; **Swanflight, Sssh!; Telling Tales,** all Roundabout Theatre, Nottingham; **People Like Us,** Pyramid Theatre Company; **In Bed With Magritte,** Royal National Theatre Studio;

(im)patience, Haymarket Studio, Basingstoke; **Telephone Belles,** Man in the Moon; **Traffic Hearts,** Man in the Moon.
Radio includes: **Melt,** BBC Radio
Television includes: **Drive,** BBC Television; **Love Bug 2000,** United Media; **London Bridge** (16 episodes), Carlton; **Sweet,** Carlton Capital Lives.

JACOB MURRAY

Theatre includes: **Much Ado About Nothing,** Arden School Theatre; **The Glass Menagerie; Nobody Here But Us Chickens,** Minerva Theatre Chichester; **On The Verge,** White Bear; **Lady Windermere's Fan; A Woman, A Dog, A Walnut Tree,** New Writing Festival (Four Plays); **The Business of Murder; Robinson's Walk,** Wolsey Theatre, Ipswich; **Victory Morning,** Bridewell; **Guerilla,** Man in the Moon and Edinburgh Festival; **Dream Children,** Edinburgh Festival.
Radio includes: **Effi Briest,** Assistant, Realize Limited for BBC; **Peronella;** News From the Front, BBC Ipswich.

LOUISE ANN WILSON

Theatre includes: **House,** Site specific,
WILSONWILSONCOMPANY by Simon Armitage; **Some Voices,** Live Theatre Newcastle; **Of Mice and Men,** Midsommer Actors; **Ten Tiny Toes,** Sherman Theatre, Cardiff; **The Other War; The Song from the Sea; All the Helicopter Night; How High is Up?,** West
Yorkshire Playhouse Schools' Company; **Three Girls in Blue,** White Bear; **Services,** The Gate; **Falling Angels,** Meeting Ground Theatre; **Natural Forces** and **The Edible City,** Humberside TIE; **Rites Rules Wrongs,** Park Tunnel Nottingham.
Assistant design includes: **Summer Holiday,** Hammersmith Apollo and Blackpool Opera House; **Uncle Vanya,** RSC, Young Vic; **Xerxes,** Bayerstadt Opera House Munich.
Film includes: **Byrons Mine,** Central Television; **Sweet Life,** Anglia Television.

FRANCIS WATSON

For the Chelsea Centre: **Room to Let,** The Chelsea Centre
Sound design includes: **Rhinoceros,** Man in the Moon; **Fossil Woman,** Lyric Studio; **Pippin** Theatremanufaktur, Berlin; **The Little Prince,** Young Vic Studio; **Candide, Danton's Death** and **Woyzeck,** all Gate Theatre; Bristol Express Play readings; seasons at the Place Theatre.
Francis has taught Lighting and Sound design at Mountview Theatre School for 2 years.
Direction includes: **Twelfth Night,** HarlekinArt Festival, Metz, France; Union Chapel Youth Theatre, **Les Femmes Savantes;** Rose Bruford College.

The Chelsea Centre
Real people, real issues, real theatre

The Chelsea Centre develops and presents new
plays of high literary value dealing with the
issues of today. It is committed to developing
new audiences particularly those not usually well
served by theatre. Over the last eighteen months the Chelsea Centre
has presented world premieres of a number of new plays including:

De Profundis by Merlin Holland
Firestarting by Julie Everton
Home Body by Tony Kushner
Just, Not Fair by Jim Robinson
The Last Bus from Bradford by Tim Fountain
Ultraviolet by Jess Walters
Skinned by Abi Morgan
By Many Wounds by Zinnie Harris
Room to Let by Paul Tucker

In this period, the Chelsea Centre has seen two of its plays (both co-
productions with Moving Theatre) transfer to the Royal National
Theatre and to the Alley Theatre in Houston. One of its premieres has
been made into a full length feature film and the Centre has received a
prestigious Arts for Everyone Award for its **Write Now** programme.
This has enabled the Centre to commission eight new writers whose
work will be presented at the Chelsea Centre over the next three
years.

For the Chelsea Centre

Artistic Director	Francis Alexander
General Manager	David Micklem
Literary and Marketing Assistant	Kelly Maglia
Dramaturgical Consultant	Mel Kenyon
Education Manager	Lisa Mead
Bookkeeper	Barry Powles

The Chelsea Centre refurbishment project

Project Architect: Patrick Dillon Architect

In April 1998 the Chelsea Centre was awarded an Arts Council of England lottery grant to develop its plans for the refurbishment of its building. With accessibility at their core, the Centre's dynamic proposals will dramatically enhance the Centre's profile, creating a bright, airy and welcoming space for new and existing audiences. The comfort and accessibility of the building for our audiences and our performers will be reflected in a new cafe, increased gallery space, improved auditorium seating, accessible dressing rooms and enhanced sound and lighting facilities.

It is hoped that with further lottery funds the Chelsea Centre will be completely refurbished during the first half of next year with the building re-opening in autumn 2000.

If you are keen to find our more about the Chelsea Centre's refurbishment proposals please call David Micklem on 0171 352 1967 or email: david.chelseacentre@btinternet.com

The Chelsea Centre Limited Board of Directors: Tim Boulton, Merrick Cockell (Chairman), Michael Constantinidi, Adrian FitzGerald, Lady Hopkins, Nigel Mullan, Eva Rausing, Janet Suzman.

The Chelsea Centre Limited is a registered charity number 1060460.

Photo simulation: Patrick Dillon Architect

Forthcoming new work

12 - 31 July at 8pm

The Chelsea Centre in association with Moving Theatre presents the world premiere of

HOME BODY/KABUL
by Tony Kushner

with Kika Markham
directed by David Esbjornson

"The dust of Kabul's blowing soil smarts lightly in my eyes
But I love her, for knowledge and love both come from the dust"
Sa'ib-l-Tabrizi

This is the story of a woman and a city. Or perhaps a love affair or obsession with a country...

It begins with a search for a party hat and ends in Kabul. In between, the entire history of Afghanistan passes before us.

Home Body looks at war, love, fantasy, guilt, Frank Sinatra and the terrible destruction of this country during our century.
From the multi-award winning writer of **Angels in America,** this is classic Kushner - provocative, funny, touching and inspirational.

The Chelsea Centre is a member of ITC

A MEMBER OF

HAPPENSTANCE

For Susan Loppert

First published in 1999 by Oberon Books Ltd.
(incorporating Absolute Classics)
521 Caledonian Road, London N7 9RH
Tel: 0171 607 3637 / Fax: 0171 607 3629
e-mail: oberon.books@btinternet.com

A catalogue record for this book is available from the British Library.

ISBN 1 84002 127 6

Cover design: Andrzej Klimowski

Typography: Richard Doust

Photograph: kT

Characters

NEESH
15, female, Indian cockney

LISA
15, female, white cockney

GALINA
85, female, white upper class, Russian descent

The action takes place in the Chelsea and Westminster Hospital; a new NHS hospital, built around a large atrium. Walkways cut across the high, airy space, joining wards and departments; large works of art hang from the ceiling and on the walls; at the base of the atrium is a café area where patients, visitors and staff mingle. Also in the central area there is a chapel, and a platform which is used as a stage for music recitals.

Speeches often overlap; a forward slash (/) in the text indicates the point at which the next speaker cuts in.

Prelude

Chelsea and Westminster Hospital, 1999. From somewhere in the hospital, music – a cello playing. A large mobile, 'Falling Leaves' – huge Matisse-type cut-outs tumbling through five floors of the hospital atrium. Galina (85, female, white upper class, Russian descent) is standing on a high walkway, looking at it. She is an outpatient, and is wearing a fur coat.

Over the cello, a collage of overlapping, recorded voices. The voices have Russian accents; sections in italics give some indication of which voices are less dominant and when.

FIRST MAN: I was sitting on the porch of the house at the trading station of Vanavara at breakfast time. I had just raised my axe to hoop a cask when suddenly in the north the sky was split in two and high above the forest the sky appeared to be covered with fire. I felt great heat as if my shirt had caught fire. I wanted to pull off my shirt and throw it away, but at that moment there was a bang / in the sky *and a mighty crash was heard.*

SECOND MAN: *There was* a deafening explosion and my friend Semenov was blown over the ground across a distance of three sazhens. At the moment when the sky opened, a hot wind, as if from a cannon, blew past the huts from the north. It damaged the onion plants. / *Sods were shaken loose from our ceilings, and glass was splintered out of the window frames. The iron hasp in the barn door had been broken.*

REPORTER: Krasnoyarets Newspaper, July 13, 1908. An extraordinary atmospheric phenomenon was noticed in this region. At 7.43 am on June 30, a noise as from a strong wind was heard followed immediately by a fearful crash accompanied by a subterranean shock / *which caused buildings to tremble. One had the impression that some huge beam or heavy stone had possibly struck the building. This was followed by two further, equally forceful blows. The interval between the first and third blows was accompanied by* an extraordinary underground roar like the sound of a number of trains passing simultaneously over rails, *and then for five or six minutes followed a sound like artillery fire. Between 50 and 60 bangs becoming gradually fainter followed at short and almost regular intervals. A minute or so later six more distant but quite distinct bangs resounded and the ground trembled. The intensity of the first explosion may be judged by the fact that horses and people were known to have fallen and windows broken by the vibration. An eyewitness reports before the first bangs were heard, a heavenly body of fiery appearance cut across the sky from south to north, inclined to the northeast. Neither its size nor shape could be made out owing to its speed and particularly its unexpectedness. However, many people in different villages distinctly saw that when the flying object touched the horizon a huge flame shot up that cut the sky in two.*

FIRST WOMAN: Somebody strongly pushed our tent. Then it repeated again, and we fell on the ground. A loud noise came from outside – somebody rattled and knocked the tent's cover. Bright light appeared, the bright sun was shining, strong wind was blowing./ Like somebody fired a shot, and a whirlwind arrived, dancing. I saw stems without branches and leaves. *Many trees were put down. Wood bedding was burning.*

THIRD MAN: *There was a deafening thunderbolt, the ground started to tremble and sway, and a ferocious gust of wind toppled the tent.* I saw trees falling, their branches on fire. The dry brush and moss was burning. Suddenly a bright lightning flashed / over the hill, as if another sun suddenly went up.

FOURTH MAN: *Dogs began to howl, small children cried.* Somebody began to knock the ground below us, and to swing the tent. I got out from the sleeping bag, and began to put the clothes on, but somebody fired from a gun a lot, and pushed the earth strongly. Like somebody had fallen and hit the earth.

SECOND WOMAN: I saw the sky in the north open to the ground and fire poured out. The fire was brighter than the sun./ I ran with my head down and covered, because I was afraid stones may fall on it.

THIRD WOMAN: *We lived at Tolsty myis, over a thousand kilometre away.* The icon-lamp swung, and the lamp-oil splashed out./ The icon standing on a shelf fell.

OLD MAN: *I washed in the bath house,* I changed into a fresh shirt. I wanted to meet death clean.

FIFTH MAN: The agdy birds are as big as black grouses. They are made of iron, and their eyes are fiery. The thunder arises from their flight above the earth, and their eyes flash like lightning. The shaman called the agdy to destroy us. In the early morning they came flying down, and brought disaster to many families of the Shanyagir: some tents flew into the air, higher than the forest. From Onkoul's herd, 250 reindeer vanished without trace. We fled leaving every last one of our belongings behind. Only the agdy can live there now. I will never go back.

FOURTH WOMAN: The ground shook and incredibly prolonged roaring was heard./ *Everything round about was shrouded in smoke and* fog from burning, falling trees. *Many reindeer rushed away and were lost.* Eventually the noise died and the wind dropped, but the forest went on burning.

FIFTH WOMAN: A ball of fire appeared in the sky. *As it approached the ground, it took on a /flattened shape.*

SIXTH MAN: A flying star with a fiery tail; *its tail disappeared into the air.*

SECTION ONE

Scene 1: gob

Partway through the prelude, LISA (15, female, white cockney) enters on crutches, wearing nightwear. She has no leg plaster but clearly has difficulty moving her left leg. However, she is determined not to stay in bed all day, and seems agile with her crutches. She leans against the walkway railing, watching GALINA.

GALINA notices her, and moves away. LISA watches her go, looks briefly at the mobile, then starts watching people moving round down below. Leaning over the walkway, she starts to let a gob of saliva drop from her mouth – the line of spit stretches until it drops down onto the people floors beneath. NEESH (15, female, Indian cockney) enters, and for a moment stands at a distance, looking as LISA does the same again.

NEESH: Hit anyone?

LISA: (*Not turning.*) No.

> *Beat.*

NEESH: Your leg broken?

LISA: (*Not turning.*) No.

NEESH: Why you got those crutches then?

> *LISA lets another string of gob drop down.*

> Can I have a go with them?

LISA: Don't touch.

NEESH: Never had crutches.

> *LISA says nothing, just lets another line of gob drop.*

> I'm Neesh.

LISA: Fuck off.

NEESH: You fuck off.

LISA: I was here first.

NEESH: No you wasn't.

LISA: Yes I was.

NEESH: That woman was here / first.

LISA: Yeah, well I was here before you.

> *Beat. NEESH goes to pick up the crutches.*

I said don't touch.

> *Pause. LISA is looking at NEESH.*

You gonna gob on someone then?

NEESH: She's always here that woman.

LISA: Not got the bottle, have you?

NEESH: Ain't nothing wrong with her, ain't got no-one to visit.

LISA: Big fucking chicken.

NEESH: Just comes here and hangs round.

LISA: Big fucking girl.

NEESH: She was outside casualty this morning.

> *LISA turns back to watching the people below.*

And last Saturday. Fucking mental, you ask me.

LISA: I didn't.

> *NEESH looks at her, then comes over and stands next to her, looking down. Beat.*

NEESH: That one.

LISA: Who?

NEESH: Red hat. Dead fit.

LISA: All yours.

NEESH: Show me.

LISA: Fucking girl.

NEESH: So?

LISA lets a lump of gob drop down again.

Missed.

LISA: Fucking didn't.

NEESH: Why didn't he turn then?

LISA: Hit his cap.

Beat.

NEESH: (*About the crutches.*) Just five minutes.

LISA: Gotta gob first.

NEESH: I'll bring them back.

LISA: No you won't.

Beat.

Why *you* here, then?

NEESH: Just am.

LISA: I seen you last week.

NEESH: Visiting my mum.

LISA: Lucky you.

NEESH: Not really

LISA: She ill then, your mum?

NEESH: Might be.

LISA: Gonna die?

NEESH: (*Defensive.*) No.

LISA: I am. I'm gonna die.

NEESH: Shit.

LISA: No-one says so, no-one tells you nothing. But I am, you know?

NEESH: Shit.

LISA: Maybe only a month.

Beat.

NEESH: I've… I've gotta go.

LISA: No you ain't.

NEESH: I'll be back tomorrow.

LISA: No you won't.

Pause – NEESH doesn't know what to say. She is looking at LISA – LISA meets her stare, challenging. Suddenly, NEESH turns and gobs onto someone far below – spitting, rather than just letting it drop. They see someone turning, looking up at them.

LISA/NEESH: Shit!

NEESH runs off, leaving LISA about to pick up her crutches when her left leg seems to buckle under her – she grabs for the rail to catch her balance, knocking her crutches to the floor.

Scene 2: samosa

Next day. LISA as before, the walkway by the mobile, standing looking down, crutches by her side. NEESH sidles up, holding out a samosa.

NEESH: Want some?

LISA: What is it?

NEESH: My aunt made it.

LISA: Fucking Paki food?

NEESH: It ain't fucking Paki food.

LISA: Smells like it.

NEESH: Cos I ain't a fucking Paki.

LISA: Just paint that colour on, do you? Max Factor, is it?

NEESH: I'm Indian.

LISA: Same thing.

NEESH: Fucking isn't.

LISA: Same difference then.

Beat.

NEESH: So you want some, or what?

LISA: And your aunt – she wrap it in plastic herself, did she?

NEESH: No.

LISA: Saw it in your pocket.

NEESH: Liar.

LISA: Saw it in your pocket, so you're fucking sussed.

NEESH looks at LISA. LISA meets her look, then takes the samosa.

NEESH: Said I'd be back.

LISA: So have a fucking medal.

NEESH: How are you… you know, today?

LISA: Gotta have my leg off.

NEESH: Liar.

LISA: Fucking am, you know. Say there's nothing they can do to save it.

NEESH: What's wrong with it?

LISA: Just knackered really. All infected and shit – gotta cut it off before it kills me.

NEESH: You ain't gonna die from a leg.

LISA: Oh, and you're a doctor now?

NEESH: No.

LISA: Watch it on children's hospital did you? Rolf Harris tell you it was OK?

NEESH: Don't be like that.

LISA: You're the one who fucking started it. Telling me I ain't gonna die from a leg.

NEESH: Just sounds so funny, don't it?

LISA: Glad it's making you laugh. Cos from where I am I can't feel nothing, and / next week

NEESH: Shit.

LISA: ... there's not even gonna be that.

NEESH: Dunno what to say.

LISA: Didn't ask you to say nothing. Just wanted to tell you, 's all. Cos next week, that leg ain't gonna be there.

Beat.

NEESH: Like if you lose a tooth, the tooth fairy comes.

LISA: Yeah, and Santa Claus exists.

NEESH: Well, what if you lose a leg? How much d'you get then?

LISA: You're mental.

NEESH: I mean if a tooth gets 50p –

LISA: That what you got? Fifty p?

NEESH: Why, how much did you get?

LISA: Same. No, a pound.

NEESH: Liar, you didn't get nothing.

LISA: Fucking did. Every tooth I lost, got a pound.

NEESH: Yeah?

LISA: Yeah.

NEESH: Yeah, so if you get a pound for a tooth – how much d'you get for a leg?

LISA: Fucking bomb, I reckon. Couple of grand at least.

NEESH: Gotta stick it under your pillow first.

LISA: You're sick.

NEESH: Sleep all night with your leg under your pillow – wake up next day, find a couple of grand.

Beat.

We could go on holiday. Ibiza, go clubbing.

LISA: Spain – we could go Spain.

NEESH: What if I don't wanna go Spain?

LISA: It's my fucking leg, right? You'll go where I say we'll go.

NEESH: Maybe we'll meet a nice Spanish waiter. Or a bullfighter, that's what they have.

LISA: Matador.

NEESH: I knew that.

LISA: So why you say bullfighter then?

Beat.

NEESH: Didn't think you'd know what a matador was.

LISA: Snotty bitch.

NEESH: Snotty bitch yourself.

LISA: Bet your cunt stinks.

NEESH: Don't say that, that's horrible.

LISA: Thinking I wouldn't know what a matador is.

Beat.

NEESH: So we going Spain then?

LISA: Yeah, like leg fairies really exist.

Pause.

How come I ain't never seen you with them? All these other rellies?

NEESH: I ain't ever seen *you* with no-one.

LISA: Ain't got no-one, that's why. Dumped when I was a kid, weren't I? Grew up in a home.

NEESH: You shitting me?

LISA points out a woman across the way.

LISA: That one of your rellies, is it?

NEESH: No.

LISA: But she's a fucking Paki.

NEESH: I told you – I ain't a fucking Paki.

LISA: So she ain't one of your aunts?

NEESH: No.

LISA: So where are they then?

NEESH: With my mum.

LISA: Come on, let's go and see her.

NEESH: (*Quick.*) No.

LISA: Thought she might like a few more visitors.

NEESH: I've… I've already been up. She's with all the others now.

LISA: Tomorrow then?

NEESH: Yeah, we'll go up and see her / tomorrow.

LISA: Bullshit.

NEESH: I've got to go.

LISA: You've always gotta / go.

NEESH: Next time, maybe?

LISA: Wouldn't she like me?

NEESH: See you.

NEESH goes. LISA watches her.

Scene 3: chapel

Next day. The girls are in the hospital chapel, in front of a large picture above the altar – Veronese's 'Resurrection'.

NEESH: Gives me the creeps.

LISA: I like it / here.

NEESH: Chapels and vicars and shit.

LISA: Quiet.

NEESH: Give me the fucking creeps.

LISA: Don't your gods all have eight arms?

NEESH: No.

LISA: Yes they do. And monkey heads and everything. Now *that's* the fucking creeps.

NEESH: Who said they're my gods?

LISA: You know they are. Everyone knows they / are.

NEESH: Maybe I…

LISA: So you're fucking sussed.

NEESH: Least we don't nail people to crosses. Have a little prayer whilst the blood drips down.

LISA: Yeah? Well least our god don't wear skulls round his neck.

NEESH: You're talking shit.

LISA: I seen it in a book.

NEESH: Yeah, well I don't believe none of that.

LISA: Yeah. Well neither do I.

Beat.

NEESH: Buy us a coffee.

LISA: (*Nodding to the picture.*) Seen that?

NEESH: Shit, innit?

LISA: Worth fucking millions.

NEESH: You Miss Antiques Roadshow now? See it on telly, did you?

LISA: No.

NEESH: That all you do, ain't it? Sit round, watching telly.

LISA: When I'm not out playing football. Climbing mountains, dancing the fucking ballet.

NEESH: Sorry.

LISA: Thick fucking shit.

NEESH: So how *do* you know it's worth millions?

LISA: Read about it, didn't I? There's a sheet at the back.

NEESH: You're making it all up.

LISA: Truth.

NEESH: Come in here a lot then?

LISA: Sometimes.

NEESH: Thought you didn't believe none of that.

LISA: It's quiet, that's all. Nice.

They both look at the picture.

NEESH: He meant to be dead then or sommat?

LISA: Think so.

NEESH: Coming up out of a coffin. Big bright light behind him.

LISA: Be fucking weird, wouldn't it?

NEESH: Like sommat's exploded. Like the sky's on fire.

LISA: Dying then coming to life again.

NEESH: That's why it don't happen.

LISA: Fucking freak you out.

NEESH: That a dog?

LISA: Where?

NEESH: In the corner.

LISA: (*Looking.*) Can't see it.

NEESH: 'S the only thing not to be bothered.

LISA: (*Worried.*) Neesh.

NEESH: Everyone else is like running away, falling down, flattened – the dog just don't give a shit.

LISA: Neesh, I can't see it.

NEESH: In the corner, for fuck's sake. Maybe dogs do it all the time – die and come to life again.

LISA: Just colours, shapes swimming.

NEESH: We don't know, do we? Don't know what dogs / do.

LISA: Neesh, it's all gone blurred. Like the colours are all falling.

NEESH: You shitting me?

LISA: Falling to the ground.

NEESH: I'm getting someone.

LISA: (*Quick.*) Clearing now.

NEESH: Wait here.

LISA: I'm – I'm fine.

NEESH stays. Beat.

NEESH: Lise, what you got?

LISA: I've got AIDS.

NEESH: No you ain't.

LISA: Fucking have.

NEESH: You gonna die then?

LISA: Told you that, didn't I?

NEESH: You can get drugs. Mark on *EastEnders* takes drugs and he's / not gonna die.

LISA: Well I ain't Mark off *EastEnders*.

NEESH: You should ask.

LISA: Anyhow, that's how I got it. Drugs.

NEESH: Fucking liar.

LISA: Fucking ain't. Got in with the wrong crowd, that's all. Couldn't help it. Just say no.

NEESH: Bollocks.

LISA: Well how d'you think I got it? Fucking some little gay boy?

NEESH: Ain't just gay boys get it.

LISA: Says who?

NEESH: Mark off *EastEnders* ain't gay.

LISA: Mark off *EastEnders* ain't really got it, has he? He's just an actor.

NEESH: Didn't mean that.

LISA: No they can't say only gay boys get it cos that would be prejudice and you ain't meant to say that.

NEESH: But it's true.

LISA: You only get it from taking drugs and being gay.

NEESH: Right, and you really know everything? You a fucking doctor now or sommat?

LISA: I know because I've got it.

NEESH: Liar.

Beat.

Them drugs can make you live again.

LISA: Yeah? Come back from the dead?

NEESH: Come on, let's get out of here.

LISA: Big fucking explosion are they? Make my sky on fire?

NEESH: Gives me the creeps.

Beat.

LISA: Gotta write in the book.

NEESH: My dad'll be / waiting.

LISA: Everyone does. Write what you want a prayer for. Little dead babies and shit.

NEESH: Maybe I don't want a little dead baby.

LISA: That ain't even funny. (*Writing.*) 'Pray for poor little Lisa, cos she's gonna die of AIDS.'

NEESH: Thought you didn't believe that shit?

LISA: I don't, just having a laugh.

Pause.

NEESH: You ain't lying, are you? You're really gonna die.

LISA looks at her and walks past her, out the door.

Scene 4: scan

Next day. LISA and NEESH in the hospital café, sitting at a table drinking coffee. LISA still has her crutches. GALINA, dressed in her fur coat again, is standing a way off, waiting with a ticket, watching a numerical counter showing when her prescription will be ready from the pharmacy (like the numbers at a deli counter). She is humming the cello theme from the start.

LISA: It's her again.

NEESH: Where?

LISA: (*Indicating.*) Stinky knickers.

NEESH: You shouldn't say that.

LISA: Barmy bird. Always here, hanging round.

NEESH: About her stinking.

LISA: Bet she does. Knickers full of piss.

GALINA's number comes up and she goes.

NEESH: That's so / nasty.

LISA: Get to that age, all of 'em do. Shouldn't be let out the house.

Beat.

NEESH: So what d'you reckon?

LISA: I ain't meant to go out, am I?

NEESH: Thought you said no-one'd miss you?

LISA: Yeah, but I ain't even got any shoes.

NEESH: I'll bring some.

LISA: All I've got is a nightie and slippers. Can't go down the fucking dinosaur museum in them.

NEESH: So I'll bring you some clothes.

LISA: Nothing Paki. I ain't going out in Paki clothes.

NEESH: I'll bring you a / pair of jeans.

LISA: One of them sari things.

NEESH: T-shirts and stuff, a jacket.

LISA: What if –

NEESH: Come on Lise, it'll be a laugh. You, me, some dinosaurs. Chat up some boys, go for a burger or sommat. Better than hospital shit.

LISA: What about your mum though?

NEESH: I'll pop in to see her first. Tell her I've got to go early – loads of homework or that.

LISA: (*Trying to get her cup to her lips.*) You ain't gonna leave me there are you?

NEESH: Why should I wanna / do that?

LISA: Just don't, alright?

NEESH: It's kicking. I ain't gonna leave you at all.

LISA drops the coffee, spilling it everywhere. NEESH leaps to her feet.

Fucking burn me, why don't you?

LISA: My arm.

NEESH: All down my / fucking leg.

LISA: Neesh, I can't feel my arm.

NEESH: This time I *am* getting someone.

LISA: (*Quick.*) Had a brainscan today.

NEESH: (*Going.*) Yeah, right.

LISA: Check if anything's wrong. Cos they still don't know what it is, you know? Still don't know why I'm here.

NEESH: (*Stopping – sceptical.*) So what's it like? You have some nice guy do it?

LISA: That all you fucking think about?

NEESH: No.

LISA: I'm ill, someone's looking at my head, and you think I'm gonna worry about some guy?

NEESH: So was he?

LISA: It was a woman.

NEESH: Shit.

LISA: Used to be a photographer – went to art school and everything.

NEESH: What, to train to do brainscans?

LISA: Stupid. She had a kid, didn't she? Had to get a proper job. Funny, int it? Could've had pictures in galleries and stuff – 'stead she's here, photographing inside my head.

NEESH: Does it hurt?

LISA: Put you in this big fucking machine. Big white tunnel, lying on your back. Like being in a tube of polos 'cept it don't smell of mint. Can't feel nothing or anything – just makes this huge fucking noise. Roaring, roaring, like loads of trains all at once going through you.

NEESH: Don't you get earplugs or nothing?

LISA: Didn't want them. Said they could put on some music – I said I wanted to hear the noise. I wanted to hear what made pictures of my head.

Then it finished, and I said could I look at it? Woman said I weren't meant to, not till the doctor had seen it. I said what if I'm not still here then? What if I've gone and popped it, and never saw in my head?

Slice after slice she showed me. Like a knife that's gone right through. You can see eyeballs and everything, you know? But you can't read nothing else. Like you can say, that dark spot, that's a tumour. Well I can't, but doctors can, you know? Or bruising or bleeding or sommat. But you can't say, look at that dark spot. That'll be my childhood. Or, see that bright bit there? That was when I fell in love.

NEESH: Who with?

LISA: I mean all those things are in there – everything I've done, everything I've thought. You – you're in there somewhere. Pretending your aunt made that Paki food. But you see it all on a screen, and you can't see a fucking thing. Slice after slice after slice. Makes you wonder where it goes, you know? Wonder where it all hides.

Pause.

My arm's coming back now.

Beat.

NEESH: So they tell you what you got then?

LISA: Don't tell you a fucking thing.

Scene 5: dinosaur

Next day. LISA stood on the walkway again, by the mobile 'Falling Leaves'. She looks exhausted – she is really leaning on the railing for support. NEESH is by her side, a big bag on the floor.

NEESH: We can go another day if you want.

LISA: Yeah, right.

NEESH: Ain't a problem or nothing.

LISA: Just leave us.

NEESH: Wanted to see the dinosaurs, that's all. Meant to be fucking huge.

LISA holds onto her head with her hands.

Imagine being a dinosaur. Lugging all that weight around. Huge big bendy neck, yeah, and a little tennis ball on top.

LISA: I said / leave me.

NEESH: Look fucking mental, wouldn't it? Little tennis ball on top. Wonder what *they* remembered, eh? How much they could fit in that brain? You reckon they remembered who their mates were? Remembered their mum and dad? Get out the family album, have a good old chat? Or maybe it's all a blank, you know? Remember nothing at all. Like each day you wake up, it's a new day. And you're right back there, where it began.

LISA: You ain't got a mum at all, have you?

NEESH: I have.

LISA: So how come you never go to see her?

NEESH: I do.

LISA: So how come you're not there now?

NEESH: Cos I'm with you.

LISA: You just pretend, don't you? Come down the hospital cos there's nowhere else to go.

NEESH: Fuck / off.

LISA: Go on, pretend that. Both of us, pretend that.

NEESH: Don't be / stupid.

LISA: I ain't ill and you ain't got a mum. We're orphans.

NEESH: No we're / not.

LISA: We're orphans and we ain't got no-one and so we come here. Like it's our home. And / everyone

NEESH: You're weird.

LISA: ... thinks you're visiting your mum and everyone thinks I'm gonna die, and we've nicked all these clothes and crutches and stuff and just wander round here all day.

NEESH: You're / fucking weird.

LISA: Go on. It'd be a laugh.

Beat.

NEESH: You know they got killed by a comet?

LISA: Who?

NEESH: Dinosaurs.

LISA: Fell on their heads, did it? Comet, sky, snuffed it?

NEESH: (*Shaking her head.*) Hit the earth, shit in the air, plants all dead. Dinosaurs kick it.

LISA: Bollocks.

NEESH: Bollocks you.

Beat.

Lise.

LISA: Can't you give it a rest, yeah?

NEESH: You had the results of that scan?

LISA: Ain't you gonna visit your mum? Or go and see some boy?

NEESH: What's that mean?

LISA: You're always going on about boys. Matadors and doctors and boys down the burger place.

NEESH: Is that wrong?

LISA: Never said it was / wrong.

NEESH: Why, don't you like boys? Fancy *me* instead?

LISA: No.

NEESH: Reckon you're lying.

LISA: Reckon I'm not.

Beat.

Bet you wish I did though.

NEESH: Wouldn't mind.

LISA: Different to wishing –

NEESH: Wouldn't think you were weird or nothing.

LISA: Thought you wanted a boyfriend?

NEESH: So? Don't mean you can't fancy me.

LISA: In your dreams, girl

NEESH: More like in yours.

Beat.

LISA: When did you know?

NEESH: Just did, right.

LISA: Don't usually tell no-one.

NEESH: All the same to me. I mean, I ain't like that. But it's all the same to me.

Beat.

So you never been with a guy?

LISA: (*Sarcastic.*) Yeah I was raped when I was three. That's what happens in children's homes. That's why I'm a dyke.

NEESH: I didn't / mean...

LISA: Or d'you think that that would sort me? Bit of cock, turn me / around.

NEESH: Fuck / off.

LISA: 'Have I never been with a guy?' / What sort –

NEESH: Just asking.

LISA: ... of question is that?

NEESH: So you ever been with a girl, then?

LISA: I'm really tired.

NEESH: Tell me, Lise. Please.

LISA: Why you want to know this?

NEESH: Cos I thought we were mates. And I reckon
you want to tell me.

Beat.

LISA: Rachel. Now you happy?

NEESH: So did you and her...?

LISA: What?

NEESH: Did you...?

LISA: Like we were mates from the first day,
you know? New school, new mates and stuff.
Everyone's got new shoes and things, and I look
a right old tramp. Keep myself to myself, never
trust no-one at first. And Rachel just started
talking to me, saying things, making me laugh.
No-one never made me feel like that, like I was
– I dunno. Like she didn't want nothing from me,
just liked having me around.

All the girls called us lezzies and stuff, but we just
laughed, said they was all just stupid. All I wanted
was to be with her. Touch her skin. Kiss her. Like
she'd put lipstick on me, touching me, ever so soft.
Felt like my heart falling, you know? Dropping to
the ground, but never reaching.

Beat.

Then, day before my birthday, just before I was 13. Coming home from school, and my arm went numb. Just froze, you know – like it was there, but it wasn't. Like if someone gives you a dead arm, but this did it all on its own.

NEESH: (*Making the link.*) The coffee.

LISA: Then when I got home, my leg went too. All down one side of me, couldn't feel nothing at all. Rushed me into hospital, tests and shit for a week – kept saying I had a brain tumour, but couldn't find nothing at all. Then one day, it just vanished. Pillow fell off my bed, and I reached down to pick it up. Hadn't reached for nothing for days, like my arm just suddenly come back. And when I went to school again, she was gone. Nobody knew why, or what – teachers wouldn't give me an address. And that was it – never heard from her again.

> *Beat.*

Well say sommat, you cunt.

NEESH: Ain't got nothing to say.

LISA: Gonna piss off to see your mum again?

NEESH: I wanna be with you.

LISA: Oh yeah?

NEESH: Yeah.

LISA: Cos you ain't got a mum, have you?

NEESH: Fucking have.

LISA: Fucking boring cow. I told you everything.

NEESH: Never told me your scan results.

> *Beat.*

LISA: Neesh, I'm so fucking scared.

Beat. NEESH goes to hug her.

LISA: Don't. Just... don't.

They look at each other.

SECTION TWO

Scene 6: light

Next day. NEESH and LISA are sharing a fag round the side of the hospital by the casualty entrance.

LISA: I'm coming out on Tuesday.

NEESH: Yeah?

LISA: Can't find nothing wrong. Eighth wonder of the world, I am. Bit of a Carol Vorderman mystery.

NEESH: You'll be back here in a week.

LISA: Will I fuck.

NEESH: Just cos no-one knows what's wrong, don't mean nothing is.

LISA: You been watching *Children's Hospital* again?

NEESH: (*Suddenly noticing.*) She's coming over.

LISA: Who is?

NEESH: Barmy old bird.

LISA: Stinky knickers?

NEESH: (*Stubbing fag out.*) Shit.

    GALINA comes up to them.

LISA: (*To NEESH.*) What d'you do that for?

GALINA: I don't suppose you've got a light?

NEESH: Shit.

GALINA: Only I seem to have mislaid my matches.

LISA: What d'you stub that fag out for?

NEESH: What fag?

GALINA: I'm sure I brought them out with me this morning. Can't think what I could have done.

LISA: You worried she gonna tell your mum?

NEESH: No.

LISA: Then why did you / stub it out?

NEESH: Cos I wasn't thinking, right? Just did it without thinking.

LISA: (*To GALINA.*) You got a fag?

NEESH: Some part of my brain just said put it out.

GALINA: Maybe I left them inside.

LISA: How come you want a light if you ain't got no fags?

GALINA: My matches. Maybe I left my matches inside.

LISA: (*Challenging.*) You ain't got nothing wrong with you, have you?

GALINA: I beg your pardon?

LISA: We've seen you, (*To NEESH.*) ain't we?

NEESH: Lise.

LISA: Neesh!

NEESH: (*Timid.*) Yeah, we've seen you.

LISA: And?

NEESH: You come here everyday, come here for the company, don't you?

GALINA: I've fractured my wrist.

LISA: You're just some sad old cow who's hanging round waiting to die.

NEESH: Lise!

GALINA: (*Matter of fact, getting out a fag.*) I'm made of stardust.

LISA: Bollocks.

GALINA: You are too.

LISA: She's some fucking *X-Files* freak.

NEESH: You should be in bed when that stuff's on. Tuck yourself up with some cocoa.

GALINA: Didn't your mother teach you any manners?

LISA: She ain't got no mother.

NEESH: I have.

LISA: Reckons her mum's up on the wards but she ain't. She's like you – no-one and nothing, comes here to make out she's got sommat to do.

NEESH: You don't know what you're talking about.

LISA: (*To GALINA.*) Here you are.

GALINA: What?

LISA: You wanted a light.

GALINA takes the light and lights her cigarette. LISA pretends to do her shoelace up, sniffing at GALINA's knickers as she does. NEESH is watching, trying not to laugh – it seems like GALINA is oblivious.

GALINA: Clean on this morning.

LISA: I never said nothing.

GALINA: Clean on every morning. That what you wanted to know?

LISA: No.

GALINA: You should be ashamed of yourself. Sniffing an old lady's knickers.

NEESH: She didn't mean nothing by it.

GALINA: (*Holding out the packet of fags.*) So do you want one?

NEESH: Don't smoke.

LISA: Fucking do.

GALINA: Fucking does, does she? You've got a foul tongue, young lady.

LISA: Sorry.

GALINA: You think I care, do you?

NEESH: You're mad.

GALINA: Yes, I think we've established that already. Coming here with nothing wrong with me.

NEESH: We were just having a joke.

As she speaks, GALINA starts to dance a little, just a few steps, almost subconscious.

GALINA: Most amusing. Of course you get to my age, got nothing better to do than hang out in hospitals, has one? Life ends at 20, let alone 70 – that's what you think.

LISA: Never said that.

GALINA: You thought it though.

Beat. She stops dancing.

See I haven't quite lost it.

NEESH notices all GALINA's and LISA's attention is on each other – she feels a flash of jealousy, of being pushed out.

NEESH: So if you fractured your wrist today, how come you were here last week as well?

GALINA: I don't see quite how it's your business.

NEESH: Just wondered.

GALINA holds out the lighter to LISA, looking at her intently.

GALINA: Thank you for the light. You are most kind.

LISA tries to take the lighter but can't – her arm won't move. NEESH notices.

LISA: (*Quietly.*) My arm again.

NEESH gently takes the lighter off GALINA for LISA. NEESH is looking at LISA, but LISA is meeting GALINA's look.

Stay a bit.

Beat.

GALINA: Goodbye.

She goes.

Scene 7: frothy coffee

Two days later. LISA and NEESH are sat back in the café, coffees in front of them, watching GALINA come over to join them, carrying a cup. GALINA is wearing a nightdress and a dressing gown, she is now a patient on a ward.

LISA: 'Frothy coffee' – d'you hear her?

NEESH: Well it is.

LISA: Cappu-fucking-ccino

NEESH: Frothy fucking coffee.

LISA: What's your fucking problem? Want to lick her fanny?

NEESH: More up your street, ain't it?

LISA: Telling her to join us.

NEESH: She was sat there all on her own.

LISA: Yeah, well so's half the fucking hospital. Put up a notice, shall we? Let them all pull up a chair?

NEESH glares at LISA as GALINA reaches their table.

GALINA: (*Sitting down.*) People stop ringing, you know? The only person who rings me is BT to see if I'm happy with my Friends and Family. Not really, no, I tell them, but I don't know what you can do.

LISA: Yeah well, don't go thinking you're special cos Neesh ain't got no-one neither.

NEESH: Lise!

LISA: (*Still to GALINA.*) Told you, she reckons she's got a mum, but she's a lying little cow.

NEESH: Me? And who's the one who reckons she's got all these things wrong with her when she hasn't?

LISA: Fuck off.

GALINA is looking at LISA.

NEESH: Who's the one who had AIDS last week? Who's gonna lose a leg?

LISA: Eat shit.

GALINA is still looking at her; LISA is embarrassed.

She's making it up.

GALINA: A nephew – I have a nephew. In Switzerland, Geneva – lots of land.

NEESH: That where you're from?

GALINA: It's where most of the family settled. Being the oldest boy left, he has it all. Control of the estate, castle on a lake.

47

NEESH: My dad had an estate. Used to take me
  to hockey.

LISA: Not that kind, stupid. God, you're so fucking
  stupid at times.

NEESH: No I ain't.

LISA: All the family money and stuff, that's what it means.

NEESH: I knew that.

LISA: No you never.

NEESH: Fucking did.

GALINA: Me – I get an allowance. Every month, in
  return for receipts. Eighty-five years old, and they
  treat me like a girl.

LISA: So why don't you live in Switzerland then? Gotta
  be better than here.

GALINA: You've never been there, have you?

NEESH: Lise ain't never been nowhere.

LISA: Fuck off.

GALINA: The thing about Switzerland is there's nothing
  there at all. I lived there for a while, when I was
  a girl. After we left Siberia, before we came here.

LISA: Siberia!

NEESH: You from Siberia?

GALINA: Oh yes.

*She leans towards LISA, goes to put her hand on LISA's
arm; LISA pulls away sharply before GALINA can touch
her. GALINA registers, but carries on talking.*

My father was a prince.

LISA: Yeah, right.

LISA is turned away, stroking her arm as if it had been burnt. GALINA deliberately turns to NEESH; she knows she will win LISA back soon.

GALINA: We used to rule part of it, you know? Tunguska.

NEESH: That Siberia?

GALINA: Mountains and forests and lakes. There was a comet once, years ago. Crashed through the sky, hit the earth. Roaring and shaking, sky on fire. Everything flattened. Trees like little matchsticks – whoosh.

LISA: (*Picturing it.*) Shit!

GALINA turns back to LISA, pleased to have drawn her back.

GALINA: Then the communists took it all. All of it, away.

LISA: (*Meeting her look.*) The comet?

NEESH: She means the house and stuff, don't she?

LISA: (*Turning on her.*) And the estate? Like the one your dad had?

NEESH: Fuck off.

GALINA: (*Still to LISA.*) The house was enormous, you know? Eighty bedrooms, 300 staff.

LISA: (*To GALINA.*) That's an hospital, that ain't an house.

GALINA: Mountains and forests and lakes and icebergs. All the bits that hadn't been flattened when the comet hit.

LISA: (*To NEESH.*) She's making this up.

GALINA: Am I? Little one-legged AIDS girl?

LISA looks at her, then gets up to go; GALINA continues, urgently, talking directly to LISA so she won't go.

All of it, taken by the army. For the People's Republic of whatever they were called then. So Switzerland, then here.

She is looking directly at LISA; LISA is still standing, and is no longer trying to leave, but won't meet GALINA's look.

Life, you know, moves on.

NEESH: Don't you miss it?

LISA: (*Sitting down again.*) Course she fucking misses it.

GALINA: (*Pointed.*) Course I *fucking* do.

LISA: Sorry.

GALINA smiles.

GALINA: Used to see bears in the forests. And you'd hear wolves in the night.

NEESH: Shit.

GALINA: And sometimes, in the winter, it wouldn't get dark at all. Day after day after day – no nights, you know, in between. Then you went a bit further, where the fur trappers were, and you'd get these lights in the sky.

LISA: Like spaceships?

GALINA: They looked a bit like that, but they weren't.

NEESH: 'Spaceships'!

LISA: (*Hard.*) 'Estate'!

NEESH looks away, hurt, pushed out; but LISA has already turned back to GALINA.

GALINA: They'd be flashing, blue, blue-green, green. Like fireworks never ending. Or petrol in a puddle. Electric lights, pulsing through the sky.

LISA: (*Imagining, awed.*) Like they really are electric.

GALINA: But they are. Streams of charged particles, storms on the surface of the sun. Bursts that travel millions of miles, hit the top of the world and make the air sparkle.

LISA: Tunguska.

GALINA: Life's all electricity, you know. Lights, brains, microscopes. All little streams of particles, making the world go round.

GALINA is looking at LISA intently; LISA smiles awkwardly.

LISA: You don't half know a lot, don't you?

GALINA just carries on looking at her.

(*Defensive.*) What?

GALINA deliberately turns to NEESH.

GALINA: Keep your eyes open, yes?

NEESH: What for?

GALINA: Nurses. They'll be looking for me. Angry, they'll be angry, when they find out I've escaped.

LISA: (*Trying to win her attention back.*) You ain't half a bad old girl, ain't you?

GALINA: (*Still to NEESH.*) Nurses, telling you what to do.

LISA: (*Trying again.*) Fucking do your head in, don't they?

But GALINA is still giving her attention to NEESH; NEESH smiles, pleased to think she's now got the attention from LISA.

NEESH: 'S only cos they cop all the shit if someone finds you've / gone walkies.

GALINA: (*Turning to LISA.*) Siberia to Switzerland to London. You'd think I'd be able to leave the ward.

LISA: (*Grinning.*) You're like me, ain't you? Stubborn old cow.

GALINA: No.

Beat. She is looking at LISA intently, as if for a long time she's been looking for someone and she's trying to decide if LISA is the one. Again she reaches out to put her hand on LISA's arm; LISA again pulls her arm away.

I was like me first.

Scene 8: leaves

Next day. Once again, they are standing on the walkway, in front of the large mobile, 'Falling Leaves'. GALINA and LISA in nightwear, LISA still with her crutches. LISA is having a bad day; it is a struggle for her to move. GALINA is whacked out on morphine; apart from the odd ramble, though, she is extraordinarily lucid.

GALINA: Falling leaves. My favourite, this one.

NEESH: I like the fish.

GALINA: Each of them falling, falling on its own.

NEESH: Think they're wicked.

GALINA: Each of them linked to all the others.

LISA: (*Annoyed.*) Which fucking fish?

GALINA: Every leaf was there before they started, but the picture only began when they started to fall.

LISA: (*Annoyed, to GALINA.*) We're talking about the fish.

GALINA goes quiet; LISA turns to NEESH, waiting for her answer.

NEESH: (*A bit embarrassed now.*) Top floor. Flying fish.

LISA: Them? Gimme the creeps they do.

NEESH: How d'you reckon they got them there?

LISA: How should I know? Big ladder.

NEESH: Or them abseiler guys.

GALINA: (*Still looking at her leaves.*) We make connections to try and make sense.

LISA: Gimme the fucking creeps.

NEESH: Lise, they're wicked.

GALINA: And sometimes there isn't any sense. Only connections.

LISA: As if you get fish that big.

NEESH: They ain't meant to be fucking real.

GALINA: Art is pretending. Making others believe your lies. Telling them lies so they can glimpse the truth.

LISA: (*Hard.*) You Sister fucking Wendy now? Art historian nun as well as princess?

NEESH: You are so fucking rude.

GALINA: (*Urgent.*) Actually, I was a dancer. At Sadler's Wells.

LISA: This before you got your hips done?

GALINA: Three minutes on the tips of my toes – tip tip, tip tip. Hardly weighed a thing, you know? Men made me fly through the air.

LISA: (*To NEESH.*) Like your stupid fish.

NEESH: Eat shit.

GALINA: Like a comet.

LISA: (*Laughing.*) Fucking fish.

GALINA: Of course, mother had always loved dancers. Put me through ballet school before I could read. All my childhood, the house was full of dancers.

NEESH: Back in Siberia? Your mother?

GALINA: (*Shaking her head.*) When we first got to London. The Russian Ballet in exile, that's what she liked to call it. They'd come and drink tea, practise in the studio.

LISA: (*Sarcastic.*) This was all *after* the comet?

NEESH: Leave her.

LISA: Fall on your head, did it?

GALINA: Then she had to sell the house, buy a little flat in Kensington. The house became a restaurant – it's a Pizza Express now. Can't go down the Kings Road – too painful, too many memories.

Like earlier, she starts doing a few little steps.

Beautiful people dancing, mother laughing, violins. Now it's a Pizza Express.

LISA: Bull.

GALINA: Nijinsky danced there, you know? When he was here with the *Ballets Russes.* Before I was born, and they all came and stayed with mother.

LISA: Thought you were born in Siberia? Before you all moved to / London?

NEESH: Lise.

LISA: She's making the whole lot up. Barmy old bird. Stinky knickers.

GALINA: Warming up, practising – collapsed on the floor, in front of the mirrors.

GALINA stops moving.

She said you could see 20 of him, reflection after reflection – a forest of dancers, all falling to the ground at the same time. One minute dancing, the next out like a light.

NEESH: (*Entranced.*) Shit.

GALINA: Dead to the world in a coma, so they rushed him here.

LISA: I don't think so.

NEESH: For fuck's sake.

LISA: Don't think this place was built / somehow.

GALINA: The hospital that was here before.

NEESH: (*To LISA.*) See?

LISA: Well she never said that, did she?

GALINA: (*Almost starting to cry.*) And she stayed as the nurses looked after him. Day after day after day, just sat there by his side.

NEESH: You alright?

GALINA: (*To LISA.*) Then one day he just woke up. Like rising from the dead, she called it. Rose up and danced, like a whirlwind – up and down the wards.

NEESH: You imagine?

GALINA: Not putting on a show, not a thank you or anything. Didn't seem to know he was doing it.

LISA: Bullshit.

GALINA: (*Still to LISA, strong.*) Just something in his brain said dance – get up, dance.

NEESH: Up and down the wards?

GALINA: (*To NEESH now.*) Amazing isn't it, how the brain works? One minute it's saying lie still, don't function; the next it's moving your limbs, listening to a memory of music somewhere inside. Diaghilev came in – very rich, the producer. Gave all the nurses half-a-crown, gave mother one too. She always kept it, never spent it. Said it reminded her – in her head, a picture of him dancing. She said it was the most beautiful thing she'd ever seen. Soon after, she met my father; and soon after that, she had me. Right through her life – the most beautiful thing she'd seen.

LISA: So you weren't born in / Siberia…

NEESH: (*Not looking at her.*) Shut it.

GALINA: Years later, they said it was epilepsy, or early schizophrenia. He spent most the rest of his life going out of his mind. Spark, spark – the body dances. Then one day those sparks start to fire in the wrong place. That's all we are – everything about us. A giant laboratory of chemicals and electricity. Brain soup and sparks; connection after connection after connection. Look in our head, that's all there is. Open up, look – all we are.

NEESH and now even LISA are silent, looking at her, somehow moved.

All my childhood, music. Mother used to rent out rooms, let people use them for lessons. When her brother stopped sending money. After my father had died.

Silence.

NEESH: I've got to / go.

GALINA: Once I was ill, pneumonia. Week after week in bed.

LISA: (*To NEESH.*) Stay a bit?

GALINA: And next door there was this woman, playing a cello. All day, day after day.

NEESH: I / need to…

GALINA: Doctors couldn't understand how I got better so quick.

LISA: (*To GALINA.*) Probably couldn't fucking wait to get away from her. Drive you mad.

NEESH: Mum'll be / wondering…

GALINA: (*Shaking her head.*) It was – it was healing.

NEESH: Mum'll…

GALINA: Beautiful. / Beautiful.

LISA: Stop lying, Neesh.

GALINA: Made me get out of bed and want to dance.

NEESH: I've got to –

LISA: You ain't got a mum.

NEESH: Fuck off.

LISA: You can stop it, this whole / pretence.

NEESH: I said –

LISA: Neesh!

NEESH: No I ain't got a fucking mum, alright? She died when I was 12. And I have to come and visit my aunt and I fucking hate her and she's marrying my dad and you happy now?

LISA: I knew you didn't.

NEESH: Never went the funeral or nothing. They said I'd just get upset, seeing her and everything. Dad just said, you'll be OK, and he went back inside. Cos I was in the garden, when he told me. '

And I sat there looking up at the sky, walls on three sides cos it was a courtyard, and this little square of sky. And the sun was bright, brighter than normal. Like it was bigger somehow, but I don't know why. And this little black bird appeared and started flying, round and round, darting from one wall to another like it was trapped, which it wasn't, but kept on darting, like it was. Then it started to rain – just gently. One drop, you know, two. Sun was shining, rain was falling. Naked rain, we call it. Sparkling like diamonds, stardust or sommat.

And I opened my mouth and the rain fell in and the bird flew round once more and flew away. And I stood in the rain and the rain fell down and that was when I knew that she had gone.

LISA is looking at NEESH, not knowing what to say.

Happy now?

LISA: Neesh.

NEESH goes. Beat.

I didn't – I swear I / didn't know.

GALINA: When my mother got ill, I wanted music.

LISA: Just drop it, will you?

GALINA: Someone to play for her, tunes she once loved to hear.

LISA: I / really don't care.

GALINA: Nobody, none of our old friends wanted to know. People with money, they are like that. You lose your inheritance, they lose their address book.

LISA goes to go after NEESH, but finds her legs won't move. GALINA carries on – there is an urgency to her voice, a need to tell this whilst she still can, a need to tell it to LISA.

No-one to come and play music. No-one to come and look after her. I nursed her myself for years, you know.

LISA stops, her back to her.

LISA: So have a fucking / medal.

GALINA: At home, the apartment in Kensington.

LISA: (*Turning, banging her chest.*) Have a fucking row.

GALINA: She'd shout and complain and refuse to eat what I cooked. And when anyone came to the door, she'd speak to them in her mother tongue. Tell everyone she was a princess, and to look at her now.

LISA can feel the urgency; she doesn't understand it, maybe it scares her. GALINA starts to reach out a hand, just a fraction. LISA flinches, almost imperceptibly, but enough to stop GALINA reaching. LISA's eyes are fixed on her, though, listening.

Then she didn't even remember that – just pulled, pulled away. Retreated into a world that was all her own. Oh I tried, I tried to reach her. Be there, where she was. But any time I got near, she just pulled further away. Didn't eat, just drank black tea. Slept for hours on end and pissed the bed.

Then one Sunday, she wasn't there any more. I went out to church in the morning, and when I got back she was gone. And I cleaned her up and bathed her and she didn't smell of piss any more. She smelled of my childhood. Like my life had gone full circle, and I was back, back where I began.

Almost everything, you know? All here before we started. Almost all the things in our head, they're there before we are born. Don't know how to use them, but they're all there, waiting. Like every egg you'll ever produce is there when you're still in the womb. Every atom on the earth, you know, just keeps coming round again.

That comet, that was new stuff. But that's once in a thousand years. Everything else has been here, waiting since the world began. What we're made of made up Stalin. Nijinsky, Henry VIII's axeman. What we're made of made up the dinosaurs. What we're made of began inside a star.

Beat.

It's eating at my body, you know? Eating my brain away.

Beat.

Scatter me where the comet hit. Scatter me where I began.

Pause.

Hold me.

LISA is frozen.

Please. Hold me.

Their eyes meet – but LISA doesn't move.

SECTION THREE

Scene 9: chair

Three days later. Round the side of the hospital, by casualty again; NEESH is having a fag on her own. LISA comes round the corner in a wheelchair. She stays at a distance, watching. NEESH looks round. Beat.

NEESH: Cunt.

LISA: Been looking for you for / days.

NEESH: Fucking cunt.

LISA: It just came out.

NEESH: No it didn't.

LISA: Didn't mean it.

NEESH: Fucking cunt.

> *They look at each other; NEESH takes a drag, looks away, then turns back to LISA.*

You want a family so much, you can have mine. Dad, auntie – all of them. Just leave me my mum.

LISA: Give us a drag.

NEESH: And don't expect me to feel sorry for you, just cos you're in a fucking chair.

LISA: I don't.

NEESH: Bet you don't even need it. Just nicked it for a laugh.

LISA: Yeah right.

> *Beat.*

NEESH: Legs packed up completely / now?

LISA: No.

NEESH: Fashion statement is it?

LISA: I've missed you, you stupid cunt.

NEESH: Don't call me a / cunt.

LISA: You called me one first.

NEESH: Cos you are.

> *Beat.*

LISA: You gonna give me that drag now?

NEESH: Lise.

LISA: Please?

NEESH: Lisa – what have you / got?

LISA: Don't.

NEESH: I want to / know.

LISA: I ain't gonna be 'that little girl with this', or 'that little girl with that'. I ain't no little girl with nothing, right?

> *Beat.*

> I'm Lise.

> *Pause.*

> And I'm sorry about your mum.

NEESH: You had no fucking right.

LISA: You gonna give us / a drag?

NEESH: Get your own.

LISA: Got no money.

NEESH: So?

Beat.

I'm gonna go see barmy bird.

LISA: No you ain't.

NEESH: You made me look a real tit / in front of her.

LISA: You ain't gonna see her.

NEESH: Don't you tell me what I can do.

LISA: Neesh, you ain't gonna see her.

NEESH: Better than talking to you.

LISA: She's dead.

NEESH: Lying cunt.

LISA: Died three days ago. Night you walked off.

Pause.

NEESH: Well it ain't my fucking fault.

LISA: Never said –

NEESH: Shit.

Beat.

LISA: Just fell, she did. Like a drop of rain. Like a leaf. Hold me, she said. Please. Then she was gone. And I just looked, looked at her. And I saw me.

NEESH: Yeah right.

LISA: Like she knew she was gonna die, you know? Knew that she couldn't be long. Like that's why she'd kept coming here; not just for tests and stuff, but for casualty things.

NEESH: But / why?

LISA: Like it was really important to die here, you know? Where her mum brought that dancer guy, up and down the wards.

NEESH: Don't make / any sense.

LISA: Like maybe she thought if she died here, I dunno. She might rise again.

NEESH: (*Sarcastic.*) Reborn as a ballet?

LISA: Or a tree or sommat. In spring.

NEESH: You on tablets?

LISA: And I thought – if that's death, then I ain't scared no more. And then I thought, really clear – I ain't gonna die. Scared me shitless, watching her. But I knew, I ain't gonna die.

Pause.

'Scatter me where the comet hit. Scatter me where I began.'

NEESH: She said that?

LISA: Like somehow she began here, but she didn't. She began, you know. Before.

NEESH: The most beautiful.

LISA: (*Smiling.*) Stardust.

Beat.

Imagine us taking her, eh? Taking her all the way there.

NEESH: Be a right laugh, wouldn't it?

LISA: Fucking mental, you ask me.

NEESH: I didn't.

Beat.

D'you think we could / really...

LISA: Don't.

They look at each other; holding the look, they start to grin; a siren starts to wail, an ambulance getting nearer and nearer, before cutting off abruptly.

Scene 10: fridges

Three days later. The mortuary – it is dark. NEESH and LISA tentatively push the door open – LISA in her chair as before.

NEESH: We shouldn't be here.

LISA: It was open.

NEESH: Don't mean –

LISA: Means it was open.

NEESH: Come on, I don't like it. Gives me the creeps.

LISA: Smells nice, don't it?

NEESH: What are those?

LISA: Fridges.

NEESH: You said this was –

LISA: It is.

NEESH: Then why they got fridges?

LISA: Use your head.

NEESH: Can't keep food in here.

LISA: For bodies, stupid.

NEESH: Bodies?

LISA: Where did you think they went?

NEESH: You mean, in there…?

LISA: Let's look.

NEESH: (*Quick.*) No.

LISA: Go on, be a laugh.

NEESH: You're sick.

LISA: Be me one day.

NEESH: Fucking sick.

LISA: My key worker used to work in a pub.

NEESH: Let's go.

LISA: Nicked all these turkeys for Christmas, sell 'em to the punters and that. But they had nowhere to put them.

NEESH: Come on.

LISA: So he talked to this guy over the road who had a funeral parlour.

NEESH: You're so full of shit.

LISA: Kept them all in his fridges. Never told any of the punters that's where they'd been.

NEESH has pushed open another door – in a glass case of formaldehyde are baby Siamese twins.

NEESH: Look at that.

LISA: Shit.

NEESH: Got two fucking heads.

LISA: 'S not real.

NEESH: Fucking is.

LISA: Fucking shit.

NEESH: Fucking big shit.

LISA: Two fucking heads.

NEESH: Me and you that is.

LISA: Piss off.

NEESH: Joined at the hip.

LISA: Pickled in smelly stuff?

NEESH: Two fucking heads.

Beat.

Come on, let's get out of here.

Closing that door, she heads back to the entrance.

LISA: Got to find her ashes.

NEESH: Could be fucking anywhere.

LISA: Got to find them.

NEESH: Let's just go.

LISA: 'S not right. Her down here, all on her own, nobody wanting her.

NEESH: You don't know that.

LISA: Fucking do. Heard those nurses talking.

NEESH: Got to keep her here till someone claims her, that's what you said.

LISA: Yeah, but nobody's gonna come. Said they've still got ashes here from the hospital before.

NEESH: They said her nephew was coming from whatsits place. Switzerland.

LISA: Yeah, well he don't fucking want her.

NEESH: So why's he coming then?

LISA: Cos he ain't, cos they got it wrong.

NEESH: Might come.

LISA: Loads of fucking money, family houses and everything – and sends a poxy allowance to her bank each month?

NEESH: Pocket money.

LISA: Eighty-two years old.

NEESH: She said 85.

LISA: Never did.

NEESH: Fucking right. Eighty-five.

LISA: Still living off pocket money. And he wanted receipts for everything.

NEESH: Tight bastard.

LISA: Telling me. Fucking receipts. So don't think he's gonna collect her somehow. Not if he didn't even come for a funeral. Not if they can't even get in touch.

Pause.

NEESH: You reckon she made the whole thing up?

LISA: What whole thing?

NEESH: Her nephew, the big house, everything?

LISA: No way.

NEESH: First thing you said to her. She was just a sad old bag.

LISA: She wasn't.

NEESH: No rellies, no nothing. That's why no-one came.

LISA: Don't say that.

NEESH: True though.

LISA: She was a princess. Lost an whole empire.

NEESH: Yeah, and I'm the fifth Spice Girl.

LISA: Don't say that.

NEESH: Don't matter, does it?

LISA: She was a fucking princess.

   Beat.

   Up there.

NEESH: Where?

LISA: Them boxes. People's names on.

NEESH: You reckon that's the ashes?

LISA: What else is it gonna be?

NEESH: I don't know.

   Beat.

   Come on, they're too high.

LISA: Can't go now.

NEESH: Just wait round, will we, whilst I grow another
   couple of feet?

LISA: Climb up.

NEESH: This is mad.

LISA: Come on – someone'll come back soon.

   *LISA wheels herself over to beneath the shelf of ashes; NEESH
   climbs up, balancing on the chair's arms.*

   Can't you reach it?

NEESH: Gotta read the right ones, ain't I? Get the
   right box.

LISA: Don't know what her name was, though.

NEESH: Reading the dates, aren't I?

LISA: They got / dates?

NEESH: Look for the day she died.

LISA: What if there's two?

NEESH: Well, one of them's called Brian. So she must be Galina.

LISA: Galina?

NEESH: That's what it looks like. Must be Russian.

LISA: You coming down then?

NEESH: No, I love it up here. Thought I'd stay till morning.

NEESH jumps down, brown cubic cardboard box of ashes in her hand. They both look at the box in silence.

Can't believe we're doing this.

LISA: Well you can't go alone, can you?

NEESH: Says who?

LISA: 'S not right. Don't come alone, grow up alone. Can't fucking go alone.

NEESH: But what if her family –

LISA: She ain't got no fucking family. Me and you, that's it.

NEESH: Fucking funny family.

LISA: Well it's all there is.

Beat.

You, me, her. All there fucking is.

NEESH is looking at her, taking this in.

Scene 11: coriander

*Next day. NEESH is stood on the walkway where she first saw
LISA, waiting. She is wearing a coat, has a bag by her side, and is
holding the brown box of ashes. LISA appears, struggling with her
chair – it seems she has real problems with one arm now.*

NEESH: Took your fucking time.

LISA: Neesh.

NEESH: Thought maybe you'd bottled it.

LISA: I can't come.

NEESH: Lise, we've got to.

LISA: I'm too tired.

NEESH: I've made sandwiches.

LISA: Neesh – my legs don't work. Alright? Problem.

NEESH: No it ain't.

LISA: No? So, how we gonna get to Russia if my legs
    don't fucking work?

NEESH: I'll push you.

LISA: Halfway round the fucking world?

NEESH: You ain't giving up on me now.

LISA: This chair ain't gonna make it to Russia.

NEESH: Lise.

LISA: Wouldn't make it as far as South Ken.

NEESH: You ain't doing this to / me.

LISA: I'm tired. Just leave me / alone, yeah?

NEESH: But I've made fucking sandwiches. Cheese and
    things – nothing Paki.

Pause.

Come on, / Lise.

LISA: My arm went numb again this morning. And those shapes were back on my eyes. I'm so fucking scared, you know?

Beat.

NEESH: That's why I'm here.

They look at each other.

Come on, we gotta / go.

LISA: She ain't gonna know.

NEESH: (*Urgent.*) Lise – we just gotta.

LISA: Anyone'd think it was your mum in that box.

NEESH: Don't say that.

LISA: Way you're carrying on. It was some barmy old bird who kicked it. Ain't gonna bring your / mum back.

NEESH: Just wanna do it properly. Just wanna say goodbye.

Pause.

LISA: What was… what was she like?

Beat.

NEESH: When I was six, one of my uncles. Just touching me – touching, you know?

LISA: Shit.

NEESH: So I told my mum, and she told my dad. I heard 'em, shouting.

LISA: Shit.

NEESH: And I pushed the door open a little bit, just enough so I could see. And he was gonna hit her. Like he raised his arm to hit her, then let it drop. Like a / leaf.

LISA: Shit.

NEESH: That's the only picture of her I have in my head – the only thing I can remember. Every time I try to think of what she looked like, I just remember her leant back on the worktop, and his hand up above her. I look at photos of her, and it's like they're someone else.

Then I smell things, things like she smelled. Jeera, fresh coriander. Crispy bhajia frying. That's how I usually remember her, remember her as a smell. Or singing, singing a song to me. Like she was a girl in a movie. Smell of fresh coriander, singing me a song.

Pause.

LISA: Alright, we'll do it here.

NEESH: You what?

LISA: Neesh, I ain't going nowhere. We can make it up. Do it here.

NEESH: You fucking lost it, girl.

LISA: Years ago. Years.

NEESH looks at her, then pulls out a lipstick.

Where d'you get that?

NEESH: Nicked it from the shop, didn't I?

LISA: Liar.

NEESH: Little old ladies running it, never see what you're doing. Slipped it in my pocket. Brought it for you.

LISA: 'Cept I can't use my arm, can I?

NEESH: Thought I'd put it on.

LISA: Don't you think I look pretty then?

NEESH: Just shut up and don't move your mouth.

LISA looks at NEESH, then closes her mouth. NEESH slowly starts to put lipstick on her – it is painstakingly careful, sensuous. When she finishes, she looks at LISA.

LISA: Do I look beautiful now?

NEESH: You always look beautiful.

A puddle of water starts to spread round LISA's feet.

(*Alarmed.*) Lisa.

LISA: What?

NEESH: You've…

They both look.

LISA: Shit. Fucking shit.

She starts to cry.

NEESH: Now I am gonna get someone.

LISA: Neesh, there's nothing they can do. It's all just packing up – everything, packing up. Keep on trying drugs and shit, nothing makes a difference.

Beat.

I've got multiple sclerosis. My nerves are all knackered. Things get lost on the way to my brain – connections fail. Comets come off orbit. Spark spark – miss the mark.

NEESH: Can't they / do…

LISA: It'll either keep on getting worse, or go away for a while.

They look at each other.

(*Determined.*) Mine's gonna go away.

Beat.

NEESH: You're like her, ain't you? Stubborn old / cow.

LISA: No.

Beat.

LISA: I was like me first.

NEESH: Gonna let me clean you up?

LISA: Why, you got a thing about piss?

NEESH: Come on, stinky knickers. Clean clothes in my bag.

LISA: Trousers and stuff?

NEESH: No, a sari. Thought you'd look rather nice.

LISA: Better be quick.

NEESH: Ain't no hurry.

LISA: (*Dead serious.*) We got a train to catch.

NEESH grins back, and wheels her away.

Scene 12: comet

Later. Though still in the hospital, something is different. We are in their world now, a world of their creation, a soundscape of their imagination. Darkness at first – music, an Indian woman singing. Lights flickering in the distance. Sounds of a railway station.

NEESH: Are we there yet?

LISA: No.

NEESH: Is it much further?

Lights slowly come up.

LISA: Three thousand miles.

NEESH: Will the train be long?

LISA: As long as the platform.

NEESH: You're so funny.

Pause. Sound of a train.

Train pulling in. Grabbing bags, lifting you up. Man in a red coat helps, he's getting off but he's helping us on.

LISA: You fancy him?

NEESH: Train pulling away, one bag left on platform. Man in red snatching it, running, running down platform, me stretching – fingers nearly reach, train too fast. Man throwing, throwing bag – arms grasping, bag in hand. In through window. On the train.

Beat.

LISA: Are we nearly there?

A cello starts playing.

NEESH: Going through Russia. Get stopped at a checkpoint.

LISA: Have to get off the train.

NEESH: Show our passports and all that.

LISA: I ain't got a passport.

Russian voices, men, cello still playing.

NEESH: You can share mine. They don't mind all that shit in Russia. Long as you give them some Marlborough.

LISA: Wants to open our bags.

NEESH: Wonders what's in the box.

LISA: Tell him it's just sandwiches.

NEESH: Looks at us kinda hungry.

LISA: Not sandwiches, I say. Photos. Family stuff, you know?

NEESH: Gets out a photo of his own.

LISA: Wife, little daughter.

NEESH: Pretty, ain't she?

LISA: Fat little cow.

NEESH: Don't tell him that of course. Tell him she's the most beautiful.

LISA: Smiling at us now. Handing back the box.

NEESH: Got to get back on the train now.

LISA: Guard brings us some tea.

NEESH: No he don't.

Voices fade; a train going over tracks.

LISA: Does too. I saw it in a film – they have a big kettle-teapot-jug-thing and the guard brings everyone tea.

NEESH: Beds – do they have beds?

LISA: Course they have fucking beds. Ain't gonna stand up for four fucking days, are you?

NEESH: I didn't know.

LISA: Stand up all across Russia?

NEESH: Just cos you saw some poxy film.

LISA: Guard's making up the beds.

NEESH: He's nice – kind of handsome.

LISA: Smells a bit. Sweaty.

NEESH: Really nice cheekbones, though. Like he found them out in the snow.

LISA: Sitting drinking our tea.

NEESH: And vodka.

LISA: Yeah, and vodka.

NEESH: Outside, everything's dark.

LISA: Trees – big trees, forests.

NEESH: Can't see nothing though. Everything's too dark.

LISA: Open the window.

Fast wind.

NEESH: Fucking close it.

LISA: Pine needles.

NEESH: Icicles.

LISA: Everything's so – so fresh.

NEESH: Freezing my fucking fanny.

LISA: Closing the window.

NEESH: Heater's really warm.

LISA: Noisy though – rattling. Never gonna sleep with that on.

A man starts singing, in Russian.

NEESH: Tired though – try lying down.

LISA: Guard's in his room.

NEESH: Singing.

LISA: Sounds brown, like the carriage.

NEESH: Sad song, about some girl.

LISA: All sounds fucking gobbledegook to me.

NEESH: Someone he always loved, left him for a soldier.

LISA: Where you get a fucking soldier from?

NEESH: Just did, alright? And he's missing her.

LISA: (*Pointed.*) Wake up now, next morning.

NEESH: (*Disappointed.*) Lise!

LISA: Train's slowing down.

NEESH: Going uphill.

LISA: Pulling into a station.

NEESH: Guard comes back, talking to us. Dunno what he's saying.

LISA: You're the one who speaks Russian.

NEESH: Fuck do I.

LISA: Going on about soldiers.

NEESH: Pulling our cases off the overhead.

LISA: Train's stopped now – got to get out.

NEESH: Is this it, then? Is this where it landed? Where the comet came, where the trees lay flat?

They are both looking around in awe at the vastness of the perceived place. Sound very sparse, empty – wind blowing.

Is this it? Is this where it all began?

Beat – she breathes in.

Smell – smell of pine trees.

LISA: And coriander?

Beat.

NEESH: (*Smiling.*) Coriander.

The Indian woman starts to sing again as LISA starts to speak.

LISA: Frontier town, wooden. Road's all muddy, pavement's planks. Shops selling everything, pans and scarves. Furs piled high, look like carpets.

NEESH: People sitting, wrapped up. Looking.

LISA: Curious.

NEESH: Staring at me. Never seen a Paki.

LISA: You ain't a Paki.

NEESH: Tell them that.

Beat.

LISA: Helicopter. Need an helicopter.

NEESH: Says who?

LISA: Read it. Tunguska, got a book.

NEESH: (*Sarcastic.*) Didn't see it on telly?

LISA: Library, asked a nurse. Got to get an helicopter, fly to the centre.

NEESH: Ain't got enough money.

LISA: Turn out your pockets.

NEESH: Ain't got nothing. Spent it all on sandwiches.

Beat.

Turn out yours.

LISA: Ain't got none.

NEESH: No money?

LISA: No pockets.

Pause.

NEESH: Sink down, on the snow.

LISA: People looking.

NEESH: Arse freezing.

LISA: (*Suddenly.*) Half-a-crown!

NEESH: Lying there.

LISA: Not lying there, her money. Half-a-crown, that dancer man. Up and down the wards – the most beautiful. Her mother – watching, looking after, waiting.

NEESH: (*Remembering.*) Half-a-crown.

LISA: Find a man with an helicopter.

NEESH: Ex-army, left it behind.

LISA: Door stuck on with sellotape. Looks a bit dodgy.

NEESH: Scared. I'm scared.

LISA: That's why I'm here.

Beat – sound of a helicopter starting up.

NEESH: Give the man the half-crown. Tell him it's from a princess.

LISA: Princess Tunguska stinky knickers.

NEESH: Barmy old bird.

LISA: Man says half-crown's fine – buy loads round here for that.

NEESH: So we offer him a quarter, but he takes it all.

LISA: Getting into the helicopter – no seats, sit on the floor.

NEESH: Ask him for a parachute – he says he used them to cover his sofa.

LISA: Yeah, really.

NEESH: Saw it on *Changing Rooms.*

LISA: Don't think he did somehow.

NEESH: Anyhow, ain't no parachutes.

LISA: Sit on the floor, behind him.

NEESH: Engine turning, really loud.

The helicopter noise gets louder.

LISA: Like the ground's shaking.

NEESH: Like somebody's knocking it.

LISA: Like somebody's fallen over, and hit the earth.

NEESH: Roaring, roaring. Rotors turning.

LISA: Helicopter lifting, climbing into the sky.

NEESH: Forest.

LISA: Forest.

NEESH: Stretching, miles of it.

LISA: Pine trees. Telegraph poles. Tall, pointing.

NEESH: Thousands and thousands of trees, all lying, same direction.

LISA: Years ago.

NEESH: Still there.

LISA: My book / said –

NEESH: Fuck your book. Lying, same direction. Branches burnt, trunks black.

LISA: Reindeer, herds of reindeer. Running – all of them running.

Noise of fire roaring.

NEESH: Something's startled them – a big bang.

LISA: Like a gunshot.

NEESH: Running.

LISA: In the distance, the sky.

NEESH: Lights. Look at the lights.

LISA: Electric pulses.

NEESH: Jumping between particles.

LISA: Blue, blue-green, green.

NEESH: Tiny sparks, jumping.

LISA: Scatter me where the comet hit. Scatter me where I began.

NEESH: Pulling the door open.

LISA: Helicopter hovering.

NEESH: Trees here still standing. Stripped bare, blackened.

LISA: But they ain't lying down here, are they?

NEESH: Telegraph poles touching the sky.

LISA: This it? This the centre?

NEESH: This where the whole thing began?

They both look in awe at the landscape imagined far beneath. No sound.

LISA: (*Turning.*) Kiss me.

NEESH: I told you, Lise –

LISA: Just do it.

They look at each other, then kiss – hard, rough, passionate. They pull apart, look at each other, grin. NEESH opens the box of ashes, takes a huge handful and throws them up into the sky, watching them tumble down – as they fall, they turn into pastel colours falling.

NEESH: Like confetti, in't it?

The falling colours get richer, autumnal.

LISA: Falling leaves.

The falling colours become white.

NEESH: Snow.

The falling colours become silver.

LISA: Stardust.

The lights fade as the colours continue to fall and the sound of the helicopter comes back – louder and louder, then dead.

End.